Puzzle Piece Living

Kirsten Hart

D1534008

Other Titles By Kirsten Hart

BABY GIRL MURPHY, ALIAS INDENTIY
REINVENTING YOU
CHAT
CHAT FOR TEENS
CHRISTMAS CHAT
KIRSTEN HART'S BEAUTY SECRETS

PUZZLE PIECE LIVING

Contents

Dedication

I've honestly got to dedicate this whole entire book to my (human-words-can't-describe-how-wonderful-you-are) husband, Dave. Thanks for choosing *me* for this incredible journey. You make me non-stop laugh through our life together, and you're the greatest encourager ever. Let's live to be 100 and 108 years old together, K?

You were my missing puzzle piece. You complete me. I adore you.

Dump Out All The Pieces

I suppose that if I'm writing a book about Puzzle Piece Living, that I should probably be a puzzle aficionado. But I'm actually not. Just kind of never have been. I know some people hold a lot of sentimental value to puzzles. Their grandmother or great aunt used to sit with them for hours while whittling away on a 1,000 piece puzzle and eating homemade sugar cookies. That wasn't me. Neither my grandmothers nor aunts were puzzle women.

I've done a few puzzles in my lifetime. Don't get me wrong. But they frustrate me. I'd actually rather paint walls. As in painting walled rooms in a house. Painting gives immediate results and satisfaction.

See it. Paint it. Wall complete. On to another task. Quick.

I've seen folk trudge away for literally days on end with some of those massive landscape puzzles. Where one flowered piece looks exactly like the other thirty-five similarly cut flowered pieces. True puzzle people have some patience skills that are lacking in my genetic DNA. Plus, where do people that work on these ginormous puzzles *eat* their meals? Typically the kitchen or dining room table is consumed with tiny pieces spread everywhere.

But, if I had a dime for every time I've told someone, "What you're currently walking through in your life will come together and make sense....like a puzzle." Well, I'd have a *lot* of dimes!

Even though being a puzzle aficionado (*a person who is very knowledgeable and enthusiastic about an activity, subject, or pastime*) is not my forte, the whole process of assembling a puzzle to completion is a wonderful life analogy.

Our lives start off with such grand expectation. As babies entering this human existence, we literally have the rest of our lives ahead of us. Our parents are bursting with pride at our fresh, untainted, and pure lives. It's a life full of potential and possibility. As if dumping out a large thousand piece puzzle. The fresh scent of the cardboard, non-bent or undamaged pieces, spread out for all to see. Psalm 139 tells us that,

"You know me inside and out you know every bone in my body;
You know exactly how I was made, bit by bit, how I was sculpted from nothing into something. Like an open book, you watched me grow from conception to birth; all the stages of my life were spread out before you, the days of my life all prepared before I'd even lived one day."

I love the 'all of the stages of my life were spread out before you' verse. Like a ginormous puzzle dumped out, God, in his infinite wisdom can look at our freshly dumped out brand new lives, and see how every single piece will fit together. He doesn't even have to take hour after hour to painstakingly fumble with his fingers to try to sort out and fit together our mismatched 'life pieces'. He sees our completed, beautiful individual puzzle. And he smiles. It all makes perfect sense to him.

Unfortunately, we aren't able to see the full picture, yet. One day we will. One day we will look back on our lives and understand how every piece had a purpose. We will understand how those hundred plain blue sky pieces, even though they seemed so mundane, actually were needed.

So let's start at the very beginning. Dump it all out. What have you got to work with? Does it look like an unorganized mess? You've got to start somewhere. Take a deep breath. Sometimes these puzzles of our lives can seem a bit overwhelming. That's why we literally have to take life one piece at a time. Step by step.

Throughout this book, I will give you steps for putting the whole picture together. Insight to understand how a jumbled mess can actually come together to form a beautiful picture. Every little die cut piece has purpose, specific meaning, and somehow fits with every other piece.

In my experience, it has always helped to turn over all the pieces. Take a look at what you have to work with. This can be a little time consuming, but it helps you get a glimpse of the big picture. Yes, there are hundreds of pieces. Yet your creator is the one who can see the final picture. God already sees you as a finished product.

There are times when I have to attempt to think outside my limited human mind. While we are created in God's image, we are not like him in so many ways. We cannot think outside of our human time and see past our human eyes into his realm. But wouldn't that be the greatest? He is both the Alpha and Omega *at the same time.* We simply can't fathom that reality. Right now. As you're reading this, God is at the beginning of time, and also existing at the end of time. He is present in both time settings.

While we are limited to Earth's time, God is not limited by anything or anyone. He is sitting right there with you, as you are deciphering how the current fragments of your life fit together to form your overall canvas of your personal existence. And if you look way, way, *way* to the end of your human lifespan, he's *still* ahead of you in your future. Standing there waiting. And smiling.

In Acts 3:4, Jesus is referred to as 'The Author of Life'. I love that name. He is the one who holds all of our answers. And he has already written out your whole story.

There have been so many times in my own life, when the pieces just didn't seem to fit. And I suppose those times are the inspiration for writing this book. Life is filled with so many how's, why's, and why not's. As if life's puzzle is just too much, too hard, and consists of way too many pieces that don't fit. I'm here to encourage you to hang on. Dump out the box. Take the time to turn over every piece, and dig in.

Will it take a long time to figure it all out? Possibly. Will it get frustrating? Probably. Will you want to take a break and walk away from it all? Isn't that just human reality? But if you do all the right steps, and stick with it, the corners and sides will come together. You'll start to fill the spaces from the outside in, and one by one, you'll see how every piece is important, and how it all fits together so perfectly.

Your life is a beautiful picture. Designed by the Author of Life himself. No two pictures alike. No two puzzles alike. All beautifully designed individual creations.

So dump it all out. Get ready for a grand adventure. Turn over all the pieces. Grab yourself some coffee, tea, or water, and get ready to start putting all these pieces together.

Chapter Thoughts

--Are you a puzzle person? If you are, why do you like puzzles? What are your favorite types of puzzles to solve? If you aren't a puzzle person, why don't you like them? What would you rather do as a hobby?

_____
_____
_____
_____
_____
_____
_____

--What would you like your life's puzzle to look like? What do you have yet to accomplish? What has been your greatest accomplishment to date?

_____
_____
_____
_____
_____
_____
_____

--Is your puzzle a beautiful picture? What would make your puzzle more beautiful?

Is there anything missing in your puzzle?

_____
_____
_____
_____
_____
_____
_____

--What does it mean to you to be 'created in God's image'? What is his image?

_____
_____
_____
_____
_____
_____
_____

--What is your favorite name of God? My favorite is that he is the 'Author of Life'. Find the Bible reference verse for the name of God that you love. Why this name?

_____
_____
_____
_____
_____
_____
_____

--If you could journey outside of our time and space, what would you like to know about your future?

_____

_____

_____

_____

_____

_____

_____

Prayer:

Dear Jesus,

Thank you for the lives you have given us to live. We are thankful for breath, purpose, and health. As we lay our lives before you, we ask that you be the one to reveal our ultimate purpose. Guide us on our journeys, so that we may fulfill our days according to the plans you have set for us. Thank you for loving us while we were still being formed in our mother's womb. We praise and love you.

Amen

The Four Corners

I'm sure everyone has their set puzzle solving formulas. But according to tips and tricks of jigsaw puzzle solving (and my own personal experience) it's always best to start with the easiest pieces of a puzzle. Those with flat sides, and in particular those squared off corner pieces that are the easiest to recognize, and assemble. Start with your corners. They are the foundation pieces to solving a puzzle.

My husband, Dave was a singer with the group, TRUTH. And out of that same group came four guy singers that formed the group called 4-Him. They had some great hit songs, but one of their best known songs was titled, The Basics Of Life. Remember the chorus of that song?

We need to get back
To the basics of life
A heart that is pure
And a love that is blind
A faith that is fervently grounded in Christ
The hope that endures for all times
These are the basics, we need to get back
To the basics of life

To me, in our puzzle solving life skills, finding and setting the corner pieces are the basics in our life. Once those foundations are set, we can then decipher the side pieces. When the side pieces are set, then the whole outer rim of the puzzle is complete.

Once our life foundations are set and solid, everything else can be put into place. But until we have four corners identified, our puzzle pieces just remain a jumbled mess. So what are these so-called corner pieces of our lives? The above song does a nice job of outlining what our four corners need to be.

A pure heart. Sometimes that seems such an improbability to have. I always battle between the two doctrines concerning the original state of the human heart. A.) We are born into sin—therefore (even as babies) we are inherently sinful and evil. B.) We were created in the image of God. God's nature resides within us. So what *is* a pure heart? Jesus said, "Blessed are the pure in heart, for they shall see God."

I'm sure we could all come up with our own definition for a pure heart. Here is one that I found. 'Fully devoted to loving God with every part of our lives'. That's a pretty good one, and sums it up well. The Greek word for pure in Matthew 5:8 is *katharos*. It means to be "clean, blameless, and unstained from guilt."

I'm not so sure all of us (while on this earth) are going to be able to attain a perfectly clean, blameless heart. But we can sure work towards it. I wrestle with the whole thought that we can reach that perfected state while alive. But the definition that says, 'Fully devoted to loving God with every part of our lives' is something that can be a part of our everyday lives. Some denominations call that sanctification. Wholly set apart to loving God and following his will.

A love that is blind. Wouldn't that be amazing if we all actually lived that out? How would we view people if we could only 'view' through our other four senses? Blind to the color of skin. Blind to 'attractiveness' and all physical appearances? That could change the world.

We live in Branson, Missouri. We're literally just a few miles above the Arkansas/Missouri state line. Soon after we moved to this area, we learned that the KKK headquarters were just a few miles south of the Arkansas state line...*in* Arkansas. I didn't even know the KKK still *existed*. It's undeniably one of the most disgusting organizations that has ever existed.

I was in the Branson high school, working with a group of students, when I asked a sophomore boy how long he had lived in the area. He told me that when they first moved to Missouri, they lived about fifteen miles outside of Branson, in the country. One night, he said, they awoke to the KKK burning a cross *in their front yard*! This isn't the 1960's. We're talking just a few years ago. I was blown away at the hatred this young boy and his family experienced. Why? Because of the color of his skin. Dear Jesus, please give us a 'love that is blind'. Truly blind to everything but what matters. A person's heart.

I don't know how people without a relationship with Jesus make it in this world. It is my personal life foundation. I can tell you firsthand that there really is a 'peace without understanding' that comes directly from Jesus himself. Without our hope and strength that we have as Christians, I don't how one survives. If you don't have this personal foundation in your life, nothing will make sense. Your puzzle will continue to remain a pile of jumbled pieces.

Ask him to come into your life, to forgive you of all your sins, and to change your heart. He will. I promise. It will be the best decision you will ever make. It's the single most important 'foundational corner' of your life's puzzle.

'A hope that endures for all times'. Hope is the lifeblood to our spiritual survival. Hope links us to our future. It propels us forward to an unknown place of promise. Without hope, we have no reason to continue. Hope gives us light on an unknown path.

Jeremiah 29:11 is one of the most well known and loved 'hope verses' in the Bible. "For I know the plans I have for you, declares the LORD, plans for welfare and not for evil, to give you a future and a hope." Our future goes hand in hand with hope.

Hope is a feeling of expectation and a desire for a certain thing to happen. As Christians, our hope is in Jesus. The message of what he taught when he was here on Earth, and of what he promises us through his resurrection from the dead. Our 'hope that endures for all time' is that our days of trials here on Earth will end, and we will one day spend eternity with him in Heaven. We have daily hope situations, and then we have this deep 'through it all' hope for our eternal future.

That kind of hope and foundation in our lives can get us through some rough days. That's why it's an essential corner-foundation. When your foundational pieces are set, the sides seem easier to figure out, and you have your connecting pieces set in place. Now to get on to puzzle building!

Chapter Thoughts

--If you're a puzzle person, what are your tricks and methods for solving a puzzle?

_____
_____
_____
_____
_____
_____
_____

--What would you say are your top three 'basics of life'? What are your personal foundational principles?

_____
_____
_____
_____
_____
_____
_____

--In the family you were raised in, what were the foundational principles of that home? Are they different from the ones you currently have? If the same or different, why?

_____
_____
_____

_____
_____
_____
_____

--Do you think it's possible for humans to have a pure heart? Can non-believers have a pure heart? What is the difference between a pure and non-pure heart?

_____
_____
_____
_____
_____
_____
_____

--Do you view yourself more as sinful by nature, or created in Gods image by nature? Can you be equally both?

_____
_____
_____
_____
_____
_____
_____

--What do you think Jesus meant by someone being 'pure in heart'? Who is someone that you would describe as being pure in heart? How are they 'pure'? What makes them different from others?

_____
_____
_____
_____
_____
_____
_____

--What is your personal definition of sanctification?

_____
_____
_____
_____
_____
_____
_____

--Can love truly be blind? Have you witnessed an act of blind love in your lifetime?

_____
_____
_____
_____
_____
_____
_____

--Have you accepted Jesus as your personal Lord and Savior? What led you to that decision? Do you, this very moment know that if you died, you would go to

Heaven? How can you be sure of this?

_____

_____

_____

_____

_____

_____

_____

--How does hope affect your everyday life? What is your current greatest hope? Why is or isn't hope important to you?

_____

_____

_____

_____

_____

_____

_____

--What are you hoping for or expecting in this coming year?

_____

_____

_____

_____

_____

_____

_____

Prayer:

Dear Jesus,

We come to you today, thankful for all that you are. Thank you for being our solid foundation in a world that is constantly changing and unstable. We pray that as we continue to seek you, that you will purify our hearts. May we walk with blind love, loving all those that you have created. Thank you for your gift of salvation and eternal life. Thank you for giving us a hope. A hope that you will guide and direct our steps, and that we have a hope of everlasting life with you. We love and praise you.

Amen

The Box Top

It's always so pretty on the top. The perfectly completed puzzle photo. What your puzzle, upon completion, *should* look like. If you do everything correctly. The box top is our inspiration. It's our ideal. It's what we're striving for. It's our constant reference point.

We can't get so bogged down with a thousand tiny pieces all over the table that we think we can never complete the puzzle. Too hard. Too many pieces. Not enough time. And way too complicated. But the puzzle *was* whole and complete at one time. Even if it was just in the factory before a jigsaw got hold of it. It *can* be complete and whole again. (Unless you've permanently lost a piece...but that's in another chapter...)

We can't lose sight of our goals and motivation. My husband's favorite Bible verse is Galatians 6:9, "Let us not become weary in doing good, for at the proper time we will reap a harvest if we do not give up." When you feel like giving up, look at that box top. Get inspired again. Remember why you bought the puzzle in the first place. You had the goal of completing the puzzle. You were excited about it. Rekindle that excitement again.

Having hope and goals is an integral need in our lives. Without hope we give up. I remember reading an article on death row prisoners. The prison was having a horrible time trying to maintain the outlandish behaviors of their inmates. When the prisoners were questioned about what was happening, they replied that they didn't have any hope of ever getting out, or of anything good happening to them, so "why should we obey the rules?"

After the questioning, the prison changed its regulations for the death row inmates. They started receiving privilege time for good behavior. They were granted extended outdoor time. They were given little rewards in exchange for modifying their previous actions. They finally had some *hope* in their lives, and it made all the difference. The problems the prison was previously having disappeared.

Have you lost sight of your big picture? What is presently inspiring you? What is your hope? If you *don't* have any kind of inspiration in your life right now, I pray that before you finish this book, you will have found it. Your own personal reason for waking up each morning. That goal that makes you smile when you're all by yourself. Your box top completed picture.

I remember when vision boards became popular. I think Oprah was one of the first to promote these boards. Take a standard cork board, and fill it up with photos and sayings of what inspires you.

They were a constant visual reminder of your goals and dreams. Psychology Today reported that the brain patterns activated when a weightlifter lifts heavy weights are also similarly activated when the lifter just imagined (visualized) lifting weights. So the thought was that if we *visualized* our future through images, our body and mind would react as if that were actually happening to us.

I need to build myself a vision board of incredibly skinny girls eating raw vegetables. Perhaps my body will react as if I'm skinny and I will start to crave only raw vegetables.

Before you think the vision boards are all weirdo New Age gimmicks, read this verse from Proverbs. "For as he thinks in his heart, so is he." (23:7) That is in the Bible, not a New Age manual. What you are thinking about in your heart, is the way you are. If you think that nothing will ever come of your life, chances are nothing *will* come of your life. According to Proverbs 23:7, what you *think* has a lot to do with who you *are*, and who you will turn out to be.

If your life's vision board is full of seemingly far-fetched dreams, lofty goals and visions, perhaps viewing that board every day, getting those images in your heart, visualizing what your future holds, will propel you towards actualization. Ever since we read our first fairy tale (or watched our first Disney movie), isn't that what we've always wanted deep down? For our dreams to come true? For what we see in our hopes and dreams to actually come to fruition in our physical world?

If God has planted a dream in your heart, hold on to it. It may not come true this week, month, year, or even decade. But keep looking at that puzzle box top. Perhaps you're just now starting to simply pick out your corner pieces. That's okay. We're all on a different time table. And dreams aren't always immediate.

Even Moses didn't cross over into the Promised Land, like he believed he would. But he fulfilled the calling God had on his life. The final picture was different than he imagined, but God showed himself to Moses in a way no one else ever experienced. Moses' picture was complete. It was full of color and whole. There were a lot of tan sand colored pieces, but they all fit together perfectly.

"I'm not saying that I have this all together, that I have it made. But I am well on my way, reaching out for Christ, who has so wondrously reached out for me. Friends, don't get me wrong: By no means do I count myself an expert in all of this, but I've got my eye on the goal, where God is beckoning us onward—to Jesus. I'm off and running, and I'm not turning back."

Philippians 3:12-14 is such an encouraging verse. Paul was *in prison* when he wrote this. Seemingly without hope. I doubt his prison guards were giving him a questionnaire about how they could improve the behaviors of prisoners at that time. But deep down Paul knew to hold on to hope. He clung to the photo on top of the puzzle box. He saw what his future held.

Don't be so distracted by confusion, disappointment, and dead end dreams. Look for the big picture. Imagine your vision board chock full of photos of you fulfilled, and living out God's calling on your life. The puzzle will fill in and come together. Trust its maker. He knows the plans he has for you. To give you a hope and a future.

I grew up listening to CCM, Contemporary Christian Music. One of the biggest artists during the 1980's was Amy Grant. One of her popular songs was 'Thy Word'. The song title and lyrics were taken from Psalm 119. "Thy word is a lamp unto my feet, and a light unto my path".

When we're confused, and not sure what our 'box top' should look like, we are told that the Word of God will light the pathway for us. The words of the Bible will illuminate our life's path. Even when we're not sure where we're headed. How? By reading how others have walked their journeys. By the words of wisdom God gives us through his word.

Chapter Thoughts

--If your life was represented as a photo on a puzzle, what would it look like?

_____
_____
_____
_____
_____
_____
_____

--If your current puzzle photo isn't what you want, what would your _ideal_ completed puzzle look like?

_____
_____
_____
_____
_____
_____
_____

--What inspires you? Who inspires you?

_____
_____
_____
_____
_____
_____
_____

--Have you ever become 'weary in doing good'? What were the circumstances? Did you overcome the weariness? How does one do that?

_____
_____
_____
_____
_____
_____
_____

--What type of 'harvest' would you like to reap from not giving up?

_____
_____
_____
_____
_____
_____
_____

--What are your current top three goals in life? How are you currently pursuing them?

_____
_____
_____
_____
_____
_____
_____

--Do you have a vision board? Have you ever had one? What are your thoughts on them?

_____
_____
_____
_____
_____
_____
_____

--What is a dream God planted in your heart that you haven't yet shared with anyone? Would you feel comfortable sharing it with a group?

_____
_____
_____
_____
_____
_____
_____

--On a scale of 1-10, how easily are you discouraged? Why do you think this is so?

_____
_____
_____
_____
_____
_____
_____

--What words of wisdom would you give someone ten years younger than you are?

_____

_____

_____

_____

_____

_____

_____

--What is your go-to encouraging Bible verse? Why do you pick this particular verse? Do you have other favorites?

_____

_____

_____

_____

_____

_____

_____

Prayer:

God,

We come to you today, so thankful for life. So thankful that you have a complete and wonderful plan for our lives. When we get distracted, we ask that you remind us that you have a 'hope and a future' planned for us. I pray that we don't lose our joy throughout our journey. Whisper into our hearts daily how much you love us. Open our eyes to the glorious future you have designed for us to walk into. We praise and love you so much.

Amen

Solid Color Pieces

I know a lot about this chapter. So I'm excited to write it. Even though it's a chapter about all the plain-colored, monotonous, and non-descript pieces of a puzzle. I've lived a lot of those non-descript days. In fact I'm kind of in one of those moods today. So I'm in the perfect mental place to write this chapter. It seems like a run-of-the-mill ordinary, unimportant 'where is my life going' kind of day. Plus rain is in the forecast, so my state of mind and current weather will be in appropriate alignment.

I'm not trying to be a Debbie Downer, but there are days like these in our lives. I've even lived through years that made me wonder 'what was *that* year all about?' I call these periods in our lives the 'solid color pieces'.

When looking at a puzzle, you don't

pay much attention to the 30+ blue sky pieces, you focus in on the object of the puzzle. But without that vast blue sky in the background, you would have an incomplete picture. An incomplete puzzle. Each piece matters. Even the non-descript ones.

I am totally a rah-rah cheerleader for living our lives to the fullest, and fulfilling our goals in life. But sometimes we need to put an honest perspective on all of that. We will walk through blah periods in our life. Days that don't seem to make sense in the grand view of reaching our goals and dreams.

When our son Tyler was two, and Ryan was only three months old, my husband Dave was let go from his job. It was an instant overnight situation. One day he was the vocal director for a Christian TV broadcast, the next day, he found out the singers were no longer a part of the show. We had two babies we needed to clothe and provide for. He instantly started sending out resumes, and interviewing for Minister of Music positions. We had loved living in Tulsa, but a church position opened up in Ohio, and we moved.

Two months after we arrived in Ohio, the church went through a very difficult split, concerning issues that had happened before we came on the scene. We left our familiar hometown, moved across the country, and straight into a *mess*. And it was ugly.

I stayed at home to raise the boys, and it seemed like almost every day when Dave got home, there were new issues concerning the church split. We survived almost a full year, when we decided to take a week-long vacation to visit Dave's family in San Diego. Four days into our California getaway, Dave called to check in with the pastor.

"Well, since you've been gone, we've interviewed another Worship Pastor, and we're giving him your job. You're out in California interviewing at another church, right?" Dave was simply *calling the office to check in* and minutes later he was informed that he had been replaced within a matter of days.

The worst part? When we got back to Ohio, the pastor told Dave that he needed to "Make this right with the church people. Tell them that you felt led to resign from the church. And if you do that, everything will work out for you". We didn't receive any severance pay. Nothing. Jobless, again.

We often look back at that year and think, "What was *that* year all about???" Sometimes we have periods in our lives where we were simply blessed to survive. To eat, live with a roof over our heads, and have a bed to lay our head on is a blessing. God provided a year of income for our family. In our Ohio home we had some wonderful days together. We were able to make ends meet, and I had the opportunity to stay home and raise our young baby boys. *That's good stuff.*

Even though that year of our lives ended in a rather bizarre and awkward experience, it was (somehow) all part of the plan. A chapter in our journey. Were we fulfilling lifelong dreams in that year? Not necessarily. But we *lived*. Many are denied the chance to live another year of life, whether because of illness, dangerous living conditions, lack of food and healthcare, etc. It is so easy to be caught up in the whole 'bigger, better, more' aspect of life (I'm including myself in this group) that we think the solid color sky puzzle pieces are unimportant.

If we didn't have those solid, non-descript pieces of our lives, there wouldn't be any contrast from the full colored integral to the central image seemingly important puzzle pieces. Without contrast in our lives everything loses perspective. If every day of our lives consisted of only the 'highs' and bright colors, we possibly wouldn't appreciate the brilliance of having a fuchsia piece pop into our normalcy.

God tells us in Isaiah that, "As the heavens are higher than the earth, so are my ways higher than your ways and my thoughts than your thoughts." While we are here on Earth, walking out our everyday lives, God knows and sees the purpose in those 'bland' years.

His thoughts *are* higher and different from ours. That is a fact that we can't necessarily fully grasp and understand right now, but we have to trust that one day down the road (or when we ultimately reach Heaven) everything, and I truly mean *every* thing and *every* day of our lives will prove purposeful.

Moses is my favorite Biblical 'character'. I already referenced him in the Box Top chapter. There are so many life application lessons we can learn from Moses' time here on Earth. In those blah days we experience, and seemingly unimportant and non-sense making seasons, remember that Moses walked through *forty* consecutive years of wondering "what does all of this mean?" And we want to give up after a rough *week*! God is so good to give us examples of ordinary people (even if they lived thousands of years ago) that we can relate to.

Moses had a phenomenal education and upbringing. It's as if he was raised in the highest privilege in this day and age— the son of a president, monarchy or billionaire. The first forty years of his life were full of 'full color' puzzle pieces. Then all of a sudden, at 40, his life drastically changed. Those colorful puzzle pieces transformed into puzzle chunks of tan colored sand. One after another. Same, same, same. No inspiration. No excitement of dreams coming to fruition. Lots of tan colored non-descript puzzle pieces.

But when Moses turned eighty, those boring days of seemingly un-purposeful days completely changed. His puzzle of life instantly became brilliant with understanding. God would use *every single* one of Moses' days in the dessert and transform the boring into radiance. God used Moses' days in the desert as preparation for leading the Nation of Israel out into the same desert scenarios. Every day of living in that desolate environment was *used of God.*

We get frustrated when two months go by, and we haven't been promoted in our jobs, or attained recognition within our career. Imagine 14,600 *days* of doing the same thing day in and day out, without one ounce of recognition. 14,600 days of shoveling sheep dung, feeding animals, killing snakes and scorpions. I would presume none of us have walked through a period that long of pure monotony. Yet every single day, Moses was learning survival tools that would enable him to successfully lead a complete nation through a similar vast wilderness.

In those 'solid color piece' days of existence, Moses learned which snakes were safe, and which were poisonous. He learned where certain scorpions hide, and how to stay safe from a scorpion attack. I can just imagine Moses gathering groups of young Israelite boys around a pile of rocks, and teaching them about snakes, scorpions, and the ways of the desert. His monotonous days were now making sense. Not a moment wasted. Everything he learned now had a purpose.

We may not be able to come to the understanding of our days of 'solid color pieces' while we're still on this earth. And maybe we will. I Corinthians 13:12 gives us hope. "We don't yet see things clearly. We're squinting in a fog, peering through a mist. But it won't be long before the weather clears and the sun shines bright! We'll see it all then, see it all as clearly as God sees us, knowing him directly just as he knows us!" (The Message version)

That Bible verse should give us hope. Feel as if you have been walking through a boring phase in your life? Don't give up. Tired of shoveling sheep dung? Hang in there, it will all be put to use. Can't see how all of the circumstances in your life right now will make sense? You aren't seeing 'things clearly'. Perhaps it may take you forty years for all of this to make sense, *but it will.* I promise.

The verse in Isaiah is not a put down. When God told us that his ways are higher than our ways, and his thoughts higher than ours, it was to encourage us to trust in him. What we can't see, he *can.* When we don't understand the reasons for seemingly silent and unproductive seasons in our lives, he does. He is shaping us to be who he knows we can and will be. God took forty years to shape Moses into the leader of Israel. When Moses came to the end of his life, I'm sure he didn't look back on his time in the desert as wasted. I'm sure he *then* understood the "why" questions.

There might have even been days when Moses was leading the Israelites that he looked back at the simpler times in his life with a bit of longing. We're always too focused on future successes that we fail to appreciate the simplicity of seemingly mundane days. Perhaps being responsible for simply his wife, sons, himself, and a flock of sheep wasn't so bad.

If you're in the middle of your life's plain colored puzzle pieces, appreciate this time for what it is. It is a time to breathe, dream, relax, and enjoy. Don't take one moment for granted. God is molding and shaping you, even if you can't recognize it at this moment.

The future will come, and it might be

completely different than you expect. The last thing Moses thought he would be was the leader of the Israelites. Remember that he stuttered, and never thought himself someone to lead a nation. But your plain colored days could instantly change, as they did for Moses when he approached the burning bush. It might be tomorrow, it may be forty years from today. But color will come back into your life.

Chapter Thoughts

--What is your favorite way to spend a 'blah' day? Do you eat a lot of sweets? Watch endless TV? Try to lift your spirits, or simply enjoy the plain monotony?

_____
_____
_____
_____
_____
_____
_____

--When was the last time you were disappointed? What were the details? How do you personally overcome disappointment?

_____
_____
_____
_____
_____
_____
_____

--What are you basic needs in life for survival? If all of your comforts disappeared, what would you absolutely need to survive?

_____

_____
_____
_____
_____
_____
_____

--If you could choose between living a life full of consistently great days vs. a life of high highs and low lows, which would you choose? Why would you choose one over the other?

_____
_____
_____
_____
_____
_____
_____

--Do you think it's fair that we don't have infinite wisdom and insight? Would you want to know everything that your future holds, or does it give you more peace to know that it is all in God's hands?

_____
_____
_____
_____
_____
_____
_____

--At your present age, are you able to look back on periods of your life, and now understand why you walked through the so-called 'solid color' days? Give a personal life example:

_____

_____

_____

_____

_____

_____

_____

_____

Prayer:

Dear Jesus,

We praise and love you. We thank you that even in the midst of confusing and blah days, you are there. Thank you for reminding us through your word, that when we are low, you are there to pick us up. We give you our lives. We place in your hands our futures. Even if it takes 40 years for our ultimate purpose, we will wait patiently. Continue to teach us your ways. We are grateful.

Amen

Easy To Difficult

"No thanks, but thank you though" is a cute little phrase we use in our family when someone offers one of us something we really don't want, but we're still trying to remain polite. I would use this phrase if someone wanted to give me an incredibly large, difficult puzzle. Not my thing. No interest. I prefer the smaller, easy-to-finish type, preferably with fifteen or less pieces. And possibly just a toddler-style puzzle with geometric shapes. Non-challenging and simple.

How come it seems some people get easier life puzzles? Why, when we'd be perfectly happy with a kindergarten shape puzzle, do we get handed a 1000 piece 3-D 'You'll Never Solve This' jigsaw adventure? Why can't it all be easy? Why must it all be so difficult? Why can't we just stay in the Puzzle Building 101 class for the rest of our lives?

Answer? I do believe that there is a reason and purpose as to why we were born when we were, and that we each have a specific purpose to our existence at this time in history. Even if it's personally challenging. Just think about the 'puzzle builders' that were born before air conditioning, indoor plumbing, and grocery stores. They're probably looking down at us and yelling, "You all have it *so easy*! You have no idea!" And here we are complaining about our current circumstances.

Perspective is so important. While we might assume that someone else has an easier 'puzzle' than we do, we don't know everything that they *have* walked through, are currently walking through, or what their future holds. I love the American Indian proverb, "Never criticize a man until you've walked a mile in his moccasins". What may appear on the outside to be an easier life puzzle, may contain internal struggles you may never know. So you can't compare. You can only be concerned with what lies before you.

I look back on my life to what, at that time and place, appeared to be a majorly difficult scenario. Now it reminds me of an easier and simpler time. I thought the guy I dated in college was *the* one. The love of my life. The one I was going to spend forever with. When we broke up (one of the many times, actually), I remember walking out into a field behind the college auditorium and crying my eyes out with gut wrenching sobs. My life was shattered.

Twenty-nine years later, I couldn't be more thrilled with who God brought into my life as my husband. He's the perfect one. Way more 'perfect-er' than the college boyfriend. God brought my soulmate into my life. But on that day, during that evening in Tulsa Oklahoma at Oral Roberts University, I thought nothing could be worse. I thought I would never find anyone to love me. *Why was he breaking up with me? What was wrong with me? Why didn't he love me back?*

At that place and time, it felt like I was attempting to fit together the most difficult challenging puzzle given to a human being. My world was harsh and complicated. In retrospect, it was simply a beginner puzzle.

I am reminded of a bible verse. The writer of Hebrews says, "For everyone who partakes only of milk is not accustomed to the word of righteousness, for he is an infant. But solid food is for the mature, who because of practice have their senses trained to discern good and evil." As we mature in our faith, we are able to handle more. Not that God wants to pile difficulties upon our lives. He desires that we would develop deeper, rely on him more, and come to the place where we understand that what seems at the moment to be so horribly unfair, really (*really!*) will all work out.

Although it would seem easy and fun, do we actually want to live the rest of our lives doing kindergarten level challenges? Wouldn't we get intellectually stagnant?

We aren't created to be stagnant beings. We need to grow and develop. We need to get beyond consuming merely a bottle of milk. We need to move on to solid nutritious foods. Even though when we're consuming our milk, milk seems like the best tasting, most wonderful food ever. My friend, there is a whole smorgasbord of foods you would miss.

If you know about my life story, you know that I recently discovered that I had been adopted. I never knew this fact. My parents kept this information from my brother and I. By simply trying to order a copy of my birth certificate when I was forty-one, I ventured on a completely unexpected journey. My world was turned upside down. My identity completely changed. I unlocked secrets that I never knew existed.

I hired a company to search for my birth mother. They found her. I discovered that my birth mother went to Sweden in

1965 to obtain my abortion. Heavy facts. Life changing journey.

After walking through that year of discovery, and all the consequences faced surrounding those months, I can handle a lot more. No sweat. I've already walked through challenging life scenarios. I've grown into my 'big girl panties'. They fit.

So whatever lies before me in my life, I have a foundation of having completed easy, medium, difficult, *and* challenging puzzle levels already. I know they can be completed. No more milk. Bring me a T-bone.

Do I want more difficulties in order to grow deeper? To be completely honest, no. No one likes walking through tough times. No one desires to walk through pain and hardships. But the reality is that it *does* make us stronger. The key is to gain the wisdom, instead of drown in the sorrow. "Weeping may stay for the night, but joy comes in the morning." (Psalm 30:5)

Pain and sorry may seem to last forever, but joy can and will eventually come. If we don't lose heart and give up.

Unless you bought this book at one of my speaking events, and we've talked extensively one-on-one, I have no idea what you have walked through in your life. You may be battling one difficult puzzle after another, with no completion in sight. I get it. I'm sorry you have to endure. I pray that in time you will have to answers to your "why's".

I am thankful that the Bible does give us encouragement, even through those times of questioning. We need hope. And James wrote us a 'hope verse'. "Consider it all joy, my brethren, when you encounter various trials, knowing that the testing of your faith produces endurance. And let endurance have its perfect result, so that you may be perfect and complete, lacking in nothing." (James 1: 2-4)

So if nothing else, you are growing in endurance! As a non-runner-but-walker, I'll take it! Endurance is good. Better than the opposite. Endurance lets you walk (or run) longer. And you burn more calories. Win-win.

If you've just experienced easy-to-medium life challenges, I pray that the rest of your life stays that way. But *if* you encounter unexpected difficulties, hold fast to the knowledge that you will come out stronger than before. And you'll be able to take on the next challenge with more strength and gusto than the previous go around.

I've been in 'the church' my whole life. For so many years, I have heard those attending churches complain that they were being 'tested by God'. As if God was smirking in Heaven while casting upon his child a test that could never be completed.

"Why God, *why me*?" is the general thought when one is going through a so-called spiritual test.

Some of you are teachers. As a good teacher, you would never give your students a test that they weren't prepared for. Teachers painstakingly drill and repeatedly review every aspect of a test with their pupils. A good teacher wants their class to *all* pass with straight A's. When students receive good marks, it shows that the teacher has successfully done their job.

Picture God as your ultimate life teacher. He doesn't want you to fail. He wants you to succeed. What happens when you pass the test of a chapter in your textbook? You get to *move on* to the next chapter of learning. It's the same with our lives. Why would a loving God get personal thrills out of watching you suffer through tests and trials in your life? The so-called tests are doorways to future chapters of expanding your knowledge and wisdom.

You wouldn't want to be a 35 year-old kindergarten student. Only learning on a level that is elementary. God desires to expand your realm of learning, and to push you through to higher levels of spiritual education. Don't fight it. Embrace it. It is ultimately all for your good.

Chapter Thoughts

--On a scale of 1-5, how difficult is your life puzzle? Are you more frustrated, or more pleased with how your life has turned out?

_____

_____

_____

_____

_____

_____

_____

--Would you be happier with a less challenging life, or do you thrive on challenge and complexity?

_____

_____

_____

_____

_____

_____

_____

--Referring to the verse in Hebrews, what would you consider as 'milk' situations you have walked through? What scenarios, at the time, seemed incredibly difficult but in hindsight, were equivalent to 'beginner puzzle' problems?

_____

_____

_____

_____

_____

_____

_____

--Do you desire to be stretched spiritually through life challenges, or would you rather stick with simpler, easier situations? What are the benefits of walking through tough times?

_____

_____

_____

_____

_____

_____

_____

--Have you ever experienced weeping that endured for the night, and joy that came with the morning? How can you use your example to encourage others?

_____

_____

_____

_____

_____

_____

_____

--James 1:2-4 tells us that endurance has a perfect result. There is purpose to the testing of your faith. Re-read these Bible verses. How would you interpret this section for a first grader to understand?

_____
_____
_____
_____
_____
_____
_____

--What words of wisdom would you tell your 20 year-old self, knowing what challenges you have walked through. What would you say to yourself as encouragement?

_____
_____
_____
_____
_____
_____
_____

--Who was your favorite teacher? What qualities did this teacher possess that made him or her have a bigger impact on your life?

_____
_____
_____

_____

_____

_____

_____

--Have you ever endured what you felt was a spiritual test? What did you learn from that time in your life? Did you view that time as more trial, or advancement?

_____

_____

_____

_____

_____

_____

_____

-- Do you know people that seem to be going through 'tests' all the time? Are they situations they bring upon themselves, or do they see them as having opportunities to advance spiritually? How can one differentiate between the two?

_____

_____

_____

_____

_____

_____

_____

Prayer:

Dear Jesus,

Today we thank you for the promise that while weeping may endure for the night, your joy is faithful to come in the morning. Is it selfish to ask for more joy than sorrows in our lives? Continue to teach us your ways. Perfect our thoughts, that we may seek to be more like you in every circumstance we face. As we face challenges, may we draw closer to you, and lean on you more than ever. We love and praise you.

Amen

Missing Pieces

I've bought very few puzzles from thrift stores or garage sales. I'll buy clothes, and yes, shoes. I know some of you might gag a bit thinking of wearing shoes that have been *worn* by someone else. I have no problem. But a puzzle? No thanks. And yet some of you totally would. See? Different strokes for different folks.

"Why wouldn't you buy a puzzle from a thrift store, Kirsten?" Two simple words: *missing pieces.* Who wants to go through all the effort, time, and energy to painstakingly configure a multi-hundred piece puzzle only to get to the last five pieces and find them completely missing from the box? That's no fun at all.

You buy a puzzle to complete every last single piece. A puzzle with five missing pieces? Completely unacceptable. One hundred percent unfulfilling. Yet it happens. Who *are* these people that would donate or sell a puzzle that knowingly won't ever be complete? Those are cruel people.

If you're like me, I still have so many missing pieces to my life. It's frustrating sometimes. The other day I was thinking about the Michael W. Smith song, 'Place In This World'. That song came out in 1990. That was the year Dave and I got married. I remember thinking that it was a nice song, and would be great for high school students. Little did I know that twenty-five years later, I would relate to it. Even though I'm almost fifty, that song still speaks to me. And about me. Here I am at my (what I like to call) half-way point in life, and still searching for *my* place in this world.

Yes, I'm a mom, wife, grandmother. I am a singer, speaker, and Worship Pastor's wife. I know *part* of my place in this world. But it always feels as if there are pieces missing—still. What do I have yet to accomplish? Should I keep doing what I am doing now, or change careers? Should I go to real estate school? Should I go back to college to study Psychology like I have thought about? What is my purpose in the next decades of my life? What *is* my place in this world?

As a speaker, I would love to do above and beyond what I currently have booked.

I would love to speak every weekend. I would love for my speaking/ministry world to expand. But how does one get from here to *there*? Where are those missing pieces?

Perhaps you have it all together. I know some people actually do. But for the rest of us, still searching for those pieces that seem lost, I want to give all of us hope. Myself included.

It's an incredible feeling when you find something that has been lost. I had my wedding ring re-set for our tenth wedding anniversary from yellow gold to white gold. And from a cheaper 'mall' jewelry store wedding band guard to one with princess cut diamonds on the sides. Don't get me wrong, my original was a beautiful guard, but the new setting for my heart-shaped diamond was extra special. And I loved it. So much so that I didn't want it getting dirty.

I started taking my ring off whenever I was doing a household job that would potentially get dirt in my setting. I didn't want my new diamonds to get build up or dirt around them. When I did dishes, I even set it up on the kitchen counter by the dishwashing fluid. Thankfully it never fell down the garbage disposal!

It was the end of a long day. We had worked hard in the yard, planted flowers, played with our young sons, and completely enjoyed an evening of watching our Tyler play t-ball. That night when I was getting ready for bed, I realized my ring wasn't on my finger.

We headed straight out to the baseball fields, and looked everywhere possible where I could have dropped my ring. We even got one of the t-ball parents who was a police man in on the hunt. He went out to the fields later on with some other policemen and searched everywhere with their flashlights. We all came up with absolutely nothing. I was devastated.

A week later, I was pulling weeds out in our front yard. And something caught my eye. *It was my ring!* Deep in the grass! I must have put it in my pocket when I was working in the yard the previous week.

The feelings of relief were monumental. I now had the outward symbol of our marriage back on my finger. I felt whole again. And from then on, I have kept my ring on my finger—even if it has the chance of getting filthy. It would be too devastating to lose it again.

For a week my wedding ring was my missing puzzle piece. The feelings of emotional devastation of losing that precious ring my husband gave me are hard to describe—unless you have had the same thing happen to you.

When we are missing that piece in our lives, we feel incomplete. What's your missing puzzle piece? What is keeping your life from feeling whole? Is it finding a spouse to share life with? Is it your career that somehow has never taken off? Are you not where you want to be spiritually?

Sometimes it's all about timing. And timing is not one of my fortes. I know we (myself included) feel as though the *present*, this exact time in our lives, is the *right* time for things to take place and happen. Today is the perfect day for you to meet your spouse. Today is the right time for your career to take off. This is the day when reconciliation with loved ones should take place. But we cannot see beyond what our eyes physically see. We cannot know the divine 'why's' of our life's timetable.

Perhaps we need to mature more. And I can't stand that thought, honestly. Because I'm ready *now*! Timing really is everything. Looking back, our move to the Branson area in 2011 was the exact right timing.

Our youngest son, Ryan (born in 1994) moved here just before his junior year of high school. For many, that would be a tough time in their lives for a move. But he was wonderful about it, and open to the possibilities of what a new town and high school held. It was near the end of his junior year, when we were chatting together on the way home from school one day. He said, "You know I'm really glad we moved here. I probably wouldn't be the person I am today, if we had stayed in Colorado Springs." What seemingly was a hard *time* in his life to move, actually turned out to be the perfect timing for his life and future.

He is currently in an excellent TV and film media school (full paid tuition for two years). He is in the exact environment he needs to learn his lifelong craft, trade, and calling. He would never have had this opportunity if we had not moved when we did. Timing, sometimes, can be everything.

So can placement. Or place. The place where you currently are, and the place you should be. Sometimes I need to pinch myself, because I've had some great opportunities to travel and sing and speak across the world. I have heard so many people say, "I want to do what you're doing", yet they haven't set themselves up to *be* in the right place. Yes, it's been a lot of right timing, and right people (that's coming up next), but you have to be in the *place* where doors can open.

Take for example the aspiring film star. I will agree that there are those unbelievable stories of being discovered as a model or actor while someone was waiting tables. But were they waiting tables in a town of 150 people in the middle of Kansas? Most times not. They were waiting tables in Los Angeles. Where most of the film industry happens.

You can't be wanting to be a famous singer or actor and never leave your tiny town. You have to *go* to where the opportunities are most prevalent.

I (kind of) kid with singles that complain about never being able to meet anyone. I'll tell them, "You need to go to the church that has a kicking active singles group with the really hot looking singles!" If you want that missing puzzle piece so bad, you have to hunt for it! It's not going to jump up off the floor into your hand. You have to get down on all 'fours' and dig through that shag carpeting! And if your missing puzzle piece fell in the kitchen, don't go looking for it in the backyard! Go to the source.

A Bible passage that has spoken to me recently is found in I Kings. Elijah the Prophet delivered harsh words of judgement to the wicked King of Israel, and afterwards, God had him flee to the wilderness, and specifically to an area beside a brook called Cherith. You probably know this story, yes? Ravens brought him food—which I happen to think is a really cool detail. But then the brook dried up (Elijah had forewarned about this drought). The 'takeaway' for all of us (I'm sure there are many, but there's one I want to focus on) is that when the brook dried up, God told Elijah it was time to move on. Time to go to another place. He said, "Go at once to Zarephath in the region of Sidon and stay there. I have directed a widow there to supply you with food."

In order for God to continue to bless Elijah, he had to *physically go* to another new place. The same might be for you. But that depends on your calling, dreams, and what puzzle piece is missing. Perhaps the years of greatest blessing are in your next town! But don't move unless you feel God is calling you on. The key is to *listen* to God's voice and he nudges, directs, gives you peace, and calls you to move locations.

If we had stayed in any of the previous cities we have lived in, we wouldn't be where we are right now. I know that seems like an obvious observation. But if we were so set on staying in Houston (even though we no longer had a place of employment) simply because we wanted to stay in that house, or in that city, we would have missed out on the blessings of where God has currently brought us.

What God has done in our lives, because of closed doors is something we never could have planned ourselves. So often we get angered and confused when a door closes. I'm sure you've heard the saying, 'When God closes a door, he opens a window'. Sometimes all the doors remain closed and locked for a long time. And we feel stuck. No windows in sight. Yet when you're stuck in that dark hallway with no open doors or windows in sight, keep your joy. Wait for the sound of a door unlocking, and journey through the unknown and unexpected door. Move through, and move on.

We were back in our Colorado house when I saw the listing online for a Worship Pastor at First Baptist Harrison, Arkansas. The online listing said that it was a church of 1,500 members. We liked that size. And we saw that Branson was only thirty minutes away. We had been to Branson a few times prior, when we lived in Tulsa. We knew we liked the area.

When Dave sent his resume to the church, he quickly got a response. "Is this Dave Hart from TRUTH? I know you! You've stayed in my house before. This is Pastor Rob Davis, I'm a TRUTH alum, myself!"

The pastor of this church that I found online, had a link to Dave already. Dave had stayed in their home! The talks began, and within two months, and two interview trips to Harrison, Arkansas, we were putting our Colorado house up for sale, and loading up the U-Haul. After two years of searching and waiting, the door unlocked.

The Harrison and Branson door opened

up new possibilities that we never dreamed possible. Since moving to this area, we have led worship for a Bible study led by Gary McSpadden (of the Imperials and Gaither Vocal Band), and we've become great friends with Dino and Cheryl Kartsonakis (the world famous pianist). In fact, we are next-door neighbors with Dino and Cheryl. Through the Kartsonakis', we have had the opportunity to sing, minister in multiple venues, and even perform in a Branson Christmas Show with them. Doors we could have never opened on our own.

Surprise doors presented the missing puzzle pieces in our lives. Walking through trying times unlocked opportunities we never imagined possible. The right place, combined with the right people catapult you into your God-designed future.

Perhaps you can't find your missing puzzle piece, because you are surrounded by people who don't care about puzzles, and would rather sit and watch TV. Don't get me wrong, I 'love me some' television time, especially cuddled up with my hubby. But if who you surround yourself with aren't even remotely interested in your jigsaw cut cardboard, you will never complete your picture.

Some of you need to press the 'delete button' on some of your relationships. The older I get, the wiser I am about who I spend my time with. And your time is valuable, too. I can't, *can't* be around negative hope-stealing people. It drains my soul to be around negativity.

And no, I'm not so idealistic that I don't realize that part of life is having to *deal* with people like that. It's the amount of time, effort, and energy that can be spent (wasted) that is an asset drained. Choose your friends wisely. Don't want to be dragged down by talking with them on the phone? Don't answer the call. Caller ID is one of the best gifts of living in this age of technology! Use it to your advantage.

Now on the flip side, surrounding yourself with the *right* people can rapidly progress your puzzle completion. You know how in real estate, they have the phrase 'location, location, location'? Well I have one for all of you. 'Network, network, network'. We live in an age where you can almost literally get in touch with *anyone*, whether through social media or the internet. Use this to your advantage!

If you want to make your living as a singer, connect with as many people as you can who are currently doing that. If you desire to be a real estate agent, connect through social media with all the local agents you can find. Read what they are doing. How they got started. Ask them questions.

We are all key holders who are able to

unlock specific doors for people. Each of us (no matter our trade or calling in life) holds valuable life information that we can pass on to others. It's kind of the 'circle of life' scenario. While other people may hold the keys to doors you desire to enter, you also hold the key to unlocking doors some may never be able to open on their own. You help people. Other people will help you. It's a great circle...of life.

The 'trick' (if you will) is finding the right people. The right 'key holders'. When you find those people who hold Godly wisdom for you and your life's path, treat them well. Hold them dear. Don't take advantage of their relationship with you. Even if they are in a 'higher' position than you, pay for their lunch or dinner on occasion. Don't assume that it's a 'take from them' relationship. How you treat others will determine how others will treat you in return when you are in the position to be a 'giver of wisdom'.

This has turned out to be a long chapter, but hopefully filled with information that will encourage you as you piece together your life. Finding those missing pieces is invaluable. Don't just think they're lost in the shag rug forever. They'll complete the picture.

Chapter Thoughts

--What is still missing in your life?

_____
_____
_____
_____
_____
_____
_____

--Describe your place in this world. What role(s) are you fulfilling? How would the world be different if you weren't here?

_____
_____
_____
_____
_____
_____
_____

--What are your current positions in life? List everything you are, and everything you do.

_____
_____
_____
_____
_____
_____

--Have you ever misplaced or lost something of great value? What was it? How did losing that item make you feel? Did you ever find it?

_____

_____

_____

_____

_____

_____

_____

--Which, do you feel, is the most important? Timing, placement, or people? How has each played a role in your life?

_____

_____

_____

_____

_____

_____

_____

--Have you ever physically moved to a new location, knowing that God was directing you? What changed in your life as a result of that move? If you haven't experienced that kind of move, how open are you to the possibility of moving, if it were to open up new doors in your life?

_____

_____

_____

_____

_____

_____

--Have you endured a relationship with a negative hope-stealer? Are you still in that relationship? How does it make you feel to be around that person? Do you have the strength to delete that relationship in your life, if needed?

_____

_____

_____

_____

_____

_____

_____

Prayer:

Dear Jesus,

We surrender our present and our futures to you. We pray for guidance and direction in every step we take. Lord, whatever pieces are missing in our lives, we ask that today, you fill those holes in. Make us complete. We pray for godly friends and mentors in our lives. Would you bring people into our lives that are overflowing with your wisdom? May we, in return, be used to bless others with insight and knowledge that you have shown us. We thank you for your constant guiding hand. We love and praise you.

Amen

Another Set Of Eyes

We prayer walked around the house. It was a foreclosure. The list price was $53,000. It was 1992, in Tulsa, Oklahoma. We so desperately wanted a house. A home to call our own. And prayer walking was kind of the 'thing' to do back then. Especially in Tulsa.

The back door was open, so we let ourselves in to this abandoned house for sale. It was in an *okay* part of town, but we could deal with that, because it was such a great price. There weren't any toilets in the bathrooms. But that was *okay*. What were toilets, maybe $100? No problem. So we buy a few, and put them in. The floors in the bathroom were all ripped up. But that was *okay*, we could easily re-tile the floors. The best part? Original hardwood floors throughout the rest of the house.

We had no idea. Absolutely none. No clue as to the actual cost of the major renovation on this foreclosure home. But we wanted it. Bad enough to prayer walk around it. Those were the days before HGTV came on the scene. Before you were able to watch multiple home renovations, and learn how much simply moving a wall could entail and cost. It's always what's *behind* those walls, and *under* the floors that's the money pit problem. And neither of us had ever replaced a toilet in our life. Nor re-tiled a bathroom.

I'm so glad we didn't buy that place. It ended up going up for real estate auction, which was a whole 'nuther area of life in which we were completely clueless. God spared us. Even though at the time we thought it would be our perfect first home. We wanted that place *bad*.

When we're smack dab in the middle of a situation, *all* we can see is what's currently happening around us. One of the best gifts of growing older is hindsight. Honestly, even though you gain weight and wrinkles, developing hindsight through your years is a far better 'perk' of age.

Is hindsight an old fashioned sounding word? You know what it means, yes? It's the understanding of a situation or event only after it has happened or developed.

When we're putting the puzzle pieces of our lives together, we can't understand how certain areas fit, until *after* the puzzle is completed. It's the same with our lives. Only after we pass through certain seasons, can we understand the "whys".

The older I get, the easier it is for me (in the *middle* of a confusing season) to *know* that the end result will eventually make sense. I have personally walked through and witnessed enough life scenarios that were so baffling at the time that ended up making perfect sense down the road. We would never have known what to do, or where to start with completely renovating a foreclosure. And God knew that. And God stopped us from buying that property.

For the past four years, we have been searching for a home to buy here, in Branson. And we've literally had two separate houses within the past two months, with accepted contract offers. The escrow checks were at the title companies. We were good to go. The problems came with the inspections.

The 'greater' Branson area is not a place where building codes are in full force, unfortunately. The first home we had a contract on was an adorable A-frame lake log cabin. Our dream. Except that in the middle of our inspection, the inspector had us get down on the floor, so that we could physically see where the house was caving in, because there wasn't an adequate foundation. Escrow check back. Contract nullified.

Just yesterday, we found out that the patio home we were planning on buying had six windows that wouldn't stay up (they would literally *slam* down when you tried to open them), and there was no way to get them fixed. No one makes those windows any more. All the windows would have to have been replaced, and the owners said they would not do any of that work. And at $600+ a window, we weren't interested in continuing with the contract.

Why haven't we been able to find the right house to buy here? We'll know down the road. One day we'll understand why all of this is happening. It will all make perfect sense in the future. Our 'hindsight eyes' will show us the full picture. In time.

We were so disappointed and confused when Dave had a meeting with the pastor of the church he was worship leading at in Houston, Texas. Going in to church that morning, he was fully employed. By the afternoon, he learned that he had four weeks to find another position. He hadn't done anything wrong. Finances had hit rock bottom at the church, and they simply couldn't afford to pay him anymore. Your life can change with a phone call. Or a meeting with your boss.

The economic fallout had hit Houston,

and apparently the people of our church had been greatly financially affected as well. We took a whole year interviewing and looking for the next church position. When seven months of a local interim church position ended, we decided our best step was to sell our Houston house and move back into the house we owned and rented out in Colorado Springs. That was our best financial option.

We planned to take the next year or more in Colorado to do concerts, and continue to look for the right church position. Our sons went back to friends they had missed. We were able to live once again in the house we built. It was the right move. After a year, we found the current church position that my husband is in. Sold the Colorado Springs house within a week, and moved to Branson.

The hindsight part of this whole story? Our son Tyler stayed in Colorado Springs to attend the University Of Colorado Colorado Springs (UCCS). It was while at this University, that he became interested in ROTC. That interest led him to signing up to join the Army. That decision led to his meeting his wife (who also happened to sign up for the Army on the same day). They are now happily married, thriving in the Army, and we have a precious grandson.

If *all* of the craziness of being let go

from our Houston church, and all the various interviews that eventually led us *back* to Colorado Springs, was all *just* for our son to find his career/calling and his precious wife, then it was all worth it. Every confusing day of that season was worth it for our boy.

His place was to be back in Colorado Springs. And if what we had to walk through, complete with the wondering, confusion, disappointment, was for our son's *benefit*, then "let's do it again". That's hindsight. That's seeing with 'other eyes', and that's the beauty of how God molds and directs our lives.

Seeing with another set of eyes can also mean to see through someone else's point of view. Through *their* physical eyes and insight. And that can be very valuable in our lives as well.

Traci Vanderbush, a Facebook friend of mine posted something that I thought was extremely timely for this chapter, and I asked her if I could use what she wrote. She said yes. Here it is:

"A DREAM SHATTERED? Maybe not. About six years ago, we were having a house built. We picked the lot, picked the floorplan and carefully picked everything we wanted in it. I was super excited about the doors and cabinets that we chose. I dreamed about hosting dinners and gatherings. We prayed over the property, wrote quotes, scriptures and happy thoughts on each piece of lumber, and on the foundation. We "owned" it before we ever made a payment on it.

And then something happened. Unexpected circumstances caused us to have to back out of buying it just one week before we were supposed to close on it! A dream shattered. Disappointment. Anger. Sadness.

BUT...guess what? Today, I am SO happy that we didn't buy that house. I'm happy for all of the insecurity of transition and unexpected events. Why? Because I can never thank God enough for the journey of the last few years and what it has taught me. He strengthened my trust in Him. He proved His faithfulness. He took us to places we never dreamed possible.

I don't own a home yet, but I'm happier than I would be if I had bought one. Today, don't get tripped up over life's disappointments. I promise there is something good ahead. It's okay to cry for a bit. Those tears of sadness will turn to tears of joy."

When we're in the middle of a difficult or confusing time of our lives, it's hard to take a step out of our environment to understand what is happening. That's why we need to surround ourselves with wise, loving, Godly people.

People with a different life perspective that can help us see beyond what is directly in front of our eyes is beneficial. Sometimes our parents are the ones to provide that insight. Sometimes other family members, or a friend. No matter who is your 'go to' person is for wisdom, pick them well, watch their lives, and make sure it's someone who has a proven track record.

First Corinthians chapter thirteen verse twelve tells us that right now, we see through a glass darkly but *then* face to face. One day our hindsight will be completely perfect. We will be able to look back on every day of our lives and see how each and every moment was perfectly sculpted to get to the end result. It really all *does* fit together perfectly. Sometimes we have to step back and catch a different perspective. Perhaps that alternate view comes from a friend or loved one.

God is the Alpha and Omega. While he is perfectly present in our *now*, he is also perfectly present in our future. He's holding your completed life puzzle. He knows where those crazy shaped pieces fit. He's the Author of Life—your life!

I'm a full-fledged grandma now. Actually, my grandma name is Gramcracker. And my husband is Popsicle. So as an official Gramcracker, you can trust me when I tell you that when you are smack dab in the middle of tough times, when you struggle through confusion and disappointments, HOLD ON. Keep on going. I'll be your personal 'another set of eyes'. And as someone who has already walked through those valleys, let me reach my hand back to you and pull you through. Let's journey together.

Chapter Thoughts

--Can you look back at a time in your life, when everything seemed hopeless, but now with hindsight, you can see how God's hand was on your life and guiding you?

_____
_____
_____
_____
_____
_____
_____

--Who is your #1 'go to' person for encouragement? Why? What makes them different?

_____
_____
_____
_____
_____
_____
_____

--What is the toughest season you have walked through in your life? What did you learn about yourself? Do you view difficulties differently now?

_____

_____
_____
_____
_____
_____
_____

--What is the best life advice someone has ever given you?

_____
_____
_____
_____
_____
_____
_____

--Are you at a place in your life now, that during a season of confusion or hardship, you can stand firm, knowing that down the road it will get better and make sense? If not, what would it take to get to that place? What steps can you take?

_____
_____
_____
_____
_____
_____

Prayer:

Dear Jesus,

We thank you for opportunities to learn and grow. We ask for wisdom in all areas of our lives. Give us daily hindsight, so that we may look back on our lives, and see your guiding hand. We thank you for protection through the years. We thank you for directing our lives. We even thank you for the closed doors that protected us from the unknown. We ask for you to continue to shape us into the person you created us to be. We praise and love you.

Amen

Take A Break

AKA 'Get To Know Kirsten's Personal Downfalls' chapter. I can be intense. Intense about planning our future, and where our personal paths are headed. If I were a shrink, I could possibly go all the way back to my birth. Seriously.

I was born to my birth mother, and then 'mother-less' for two weeks prior to my adoption. As soon as I was born, I was whisked away to the infant nursery, and never allowed time to bond with my birth mother.

Some may count this as meaningless, and that I was completely loved and taken care of by my adopted parents. And that is true. But I've also learned there's a sort of fight or flight instinct that happens to orphaned babies. They realize their whole world has changed, and none of the 'comforts' (mother's sounds, etc.) are there to comfort them. They either have to 'fight' to survive in a non-comforting world, or 'flight'—sort of give up. It's actually quite fascinating. And to this day I have no idea where I was, or what was happening during my first weeks of life.

"But you weren't an orphan, Kirsten, you were adopted at two weeks old". I realize that. But yet somewhere deep down, I think I was affected by those two weeks in a way. The 'way' is that I have a strong desire to know what my future holds. I don't like the unknowing. I don't like uncertainty. My 'fight' instinct kicks in, and I want to take control of what happens to me.

And that, right there, is a difficulty when it comes to living in this world. We aren't guaranteed anything past our *present*. And as many of you know, you don't even really have control of *that*. Your life can change in an instant. In one phone call your life can be turned upside-down. We can be here one minute, and gone the next. Unfortunately I have witnessed that all too often.

So sometimes. Not necessarily all the time. But at certain times in our months, years, lifetime, we need to step back from the puzzle and take a break. Walk away from all the mumbled, jumbled pieces, and not worry so much about how every piece should fit together, and why some pieces seemingly don't fit anywhere at all. We all do it. We all need breaks.

I love taking walks. I wish I loved taking runs, but I really don't. Walks, and fast walking are more my style. Walks can take you out and away from your current situation and setting. Not that your current situation and setting is *bad*, but a different perspective, and a break from the 'norm' is always a good thing.

We live in condos that are right next to the beautiful Lake Taneycomo. It's actually more of a river, the White River to be exact, but since both ends are now (dammed) up, they changed the name from the White River to Lake Taneycomo. You can thank me later for that little river/lake history lesson. But I love my Lake Taneycomo walks.

It's probably a good mile and a half to walk the lake path completely in one direction. And I like to do it multiple times. Not necessarily because I'm such the athlete. It's really about the ducklings.

We have tons of ducks (and some pesky pooping geese) that make this area their home. But the ducklings. The *ducklings* and their mamas melt my heart. It melts my heart to be walking along the river/lake banks and stumble upon a brand new family of chocolate and butter colored fluffy tiny babies. And this year, there have been multiple new families.

Whenever I see these babies along the banks or out learning to swim with their mamas, my perspective changes. I think about how blessed I am to be able to witness new life, new purpose, and how God speaks to these creatures through their instinct. I breathe fresh air, enjoy the sunshine, and marvel at the beauty of this area. I take a break. Breaks are good.

Maybe I'm alone in wanting to plan out my future, and get the puzzle competed in record time. But I think some of you might feel the same way. It can be overwhelming. Where is the next paycheck coming from? How will I make the payments due at the end of the month? Will I get laid off like so many of my co-workers? Will my marriage ever be mended? Will the relationships with my children ever heal? Will I ever find the love of my life? Will I ever be happy again?

We are daily surrounded by so many unknowns and so much that is out of our control. There used to be a phrase that said, "Take a chill pill". Perhaps in the 60's one would take a Quaalude. In other words, take something that will help you relax, lay back, and not worry so much. Easier said than done.

When we take a break, breathe deeply, and close our eyes from the hassles and concerns of daily life, it helps us refocus.

We can't be 100% intense all the time. If we sat 24/7 in front of a thousand piece jigsaw puzzle from start to finish without taking any breaks, it could drive one crazy. It's too much. Too intense. Too much time without changing focus.

One of my favorite Bible verses is Isaiah 30:31, "But they that wait upon the Lord shall renew their strength; they shall mount up with wings as eagles; they shall run, and not be weary; and they shall walk, and not faint." Waiting and resting, yes, can be different, but also have similarities. Both give us renewed strength.

As Christians, the difference from 'taking a chill pill', and the above verse, is that we are waiting/resting *in* the Lord. We don't have the ability ourselves to find strength in waiting, but when we lean on our maker, he gives us supernatural strength to not be weary and not faint.

I love the visual of mounting up with wings as eagles. A business friend lived along the Mississippi River in Saint Louis. His house was on a high bluff overlooking the water. He sent out a memo to all his employees that told of something he had witnessed that morning. He had been out on their patio that overlooked the river, and was watching an eagle soar high above the Mississippi. As the eagle was soaring, black crows started chasing after the eagle, trying to attack it. He watched as the eagle flew higher and higher, leaving the crows at a lower altitude. Soon the crows were no longer a bother.

The biblical image of an eagle is not to be ignored. Here's an example of the superiority of an eagle. Eagles and a turkeys react very differently to the threat of a storm. A turkey runs under the barn, hoping the storm won't come near. The eagle, on the other hand, leaves the security of its nest and spreads its wings to ride the air currents of the approaching storm, knowing they will carry it higher than it could soar on its own.

When an eagle is attacked by a pack of crows it doesn't fight back. All it does is simply fly higher and higher, knowing that pretty soon the crows won't be able to fly at that altitude. The eagle plays smart rather than lose its sensibility in the mindless games of small-thinking crows.

In waiting on the Lord, he promises us that we will likewise 'mount up with wings as eagles'. We will have the ability to soar above storms and away from crows that seek to bring us down. Great analogy and promise.

We are taught that being aggressive, working harder, and not stopping will give us the leg up and advantage over others. That's why what the Bible teaches us is radically different from what the world teaches us.

Yes, we must work and be diligent, but working harder by our own strength is completely different than the principle of rest in this Isaiah passage. When we rest in God's strength, he promises us that we will have supernatural strength and wisdom—like that of the eagle.

Resting is a biblical principle that we see even from the beginning of the book of Genesis. When God was finished with initial creation, he *rested.* It seems odd to me that the one who never sleeps rested. But this is what we are told by divine inspiration. There has to be a purpose in God's resting. If nothing else, to show that it is a vital part of God's plan for our lives.

A rest, or Sabbath was ordered by God for his people. It was mandatory. It was law. It was a commandment given to Moses in the 10 Commandments. It was vital.

Jesus even told his disciples to rest. Mark 6:31 "And he said to them, "Come away by yourselves to a desolate place and rest a while." For many were coming and going, and they had no leisure even to eat." We get so wrapped up in day to day decisions and planning for our futures, that it can become overwhelming. And God knows that fact. He made us. He knows what we need to survive. And he told his disciples to go away and rest.

I want to interject that I'm not telling you to go take a month long vacation away from your spouse and children. That's not practical, or something I would recommend. Some of you might think that's a wonderful idea. But a weekend to regroup and refocus? Sounds great. That's what is so wonderful about speaking for women's retreats.

Retreats give us a break. We're in a different environment and setting. There's no food to prepare or laundry to fold. You get appointed time away to commune with your God. Perhaps I should have named this chapter 'Go On A Women's Retreat'.

Last November, my husband and I had a singing engagement in Miami Florida. I played around online for a while looking at cruises that left out of the Port of Miami. How fun would it be to tag on a cruise after our singing job? I found one that left the day after our singing date. And it was cheap. I mean dirt cheap. Because we booked it last minute (the week *before* we left to sing), it was only $100 each, for a four night, five day cruise to the Bahamas. Steal of a deal. A much needed and appreciated getaway together.

And while I wouldn't recommend taking a month away from your husband and children, I *would* highly recommend a week long cruise with your husband. No food to prepare. No laundry to worry about. Just the two of us, talking about our past year, and planning what was ahead. It was the perfect setting to chat about the blessings of the previous year, while dreaming about the future.

There's something about staring out into the vast blue ocean water that puts your life into perspective. The world is so much bigger than our tiny corner of problems. When gazing at the oceans, the grand starry sky, and the universe, our temporary trials pale in comparison to what God has planned for us. *That* kind of a break to gain perspective is valuable. And needed.

Is your life's puzzle bogging you down? Are you frustrated with working out how all those pieces will somehow fit together? Do you just want to walk away from it all? Does it seem easier to simply put the puzzle completely unfinished back in its box, and out to the garage sale pile? I understand. I really do.

They that wait upon the *Lord* shall renew their strength. There's something miraculous that happens when we wait for the Lord to speak and move. When we look to him during our times our times of rest and 'breaks', he will speak to us. That's the 'magical' (if you will...) part of being a Christian. When we want to give up because we are frustrated, he give us peace. He also is the best at giving new perspective. But we have to walk away from our puzzle for a while.

Waiting on the Lord will give us renewed strength as an eagle. Waiting on the Lord will give us the ability to run and not be weary, to walk and not faint, as we traverse along our path.

Go take a walk in the sunshine. Find a new path to hike. Ride your bike. Take a cruise. Go on a retreat getaway. Whatever it takes. Get refreshed, and jump back in. We've got a puzzle to solve!

Chapter Thoughts

--What's your favorite way to relax? Do you sleep well at night? Is it easy for you to rest?

_____

_____

_____

_____

_____

_____

_____

--If you could go anywhere on a vacation with a certain person, where would it be, and who would you take? Why that location? Why that person?

_____

_____

_____

_____

_____

_____

_____

--Are you good at waiting? Who is the most patient person you know? Who is the most impatient person you know? How are their lives different?

_____

_____

_____
_____
_____
_____
_____

--When was the last time you took a vacation? On a scale of 1-10, how badly do you need to get away from it all right now? What is currently weighing your life down?

_____
_____
_____
_____
_____
_____
_____

--Why do you think the Bible tells us that "on the seventh day God rested"? In Psalm 121:4, we are told that God does not slumber or sleep. Yet he rested. Why?

_____
_____
_____
_____
_____
_____
_____

--When Jesus told his disciples in Mark 6:31 to go to a desperate place and rest, what had they just been doing? Why would they need to go away and rest?

_____
_____
_____
_____
_____
_____
_____

--Do you ever take a full Sabbath, a full day of rest? The Sabbath was a commandment given by God. Are we 'modern day' Christians too busy to observe that commandment of God, or does it not apply to us today, and our lifestyles?

_____
_____
_____
_____
_____
_____
_____

Prayer:

Dear Jesus,

Teach us to be more like you. Teach us your ways. We ask for your wisdom in our lives. Thank you for you example of resting. Thank you for teaching us about taking a Sabbath, a full day of rest. When we get weary, we ask that you give us supernatural strength to continue on. Thank you for the promise that when we wait on you, we will be able to soar like an eagle. We love you and thank you for these promises.

Amen

I Can See It

I was born in 1966, so I totally remember the song I Can See Clearly Now by Johnny Nash. "I can see clearly now the rain is gone/I can see all obstacles in my way/Gone are the dark clouds that had me blind/It's gonna be a bright (bright), bright (bright) Sun-Shiny day." Remember it? If I've done my job correctly, you're going to have that song stuck in your head *all day long.* You're welcome.

When you near completion of your puzzle, and it all starts making sense and coming together, it becomes a 'bright Sun-Shiny day'. Accomplishment is a great feeling. It's rewarding. It makes you feel like all those painstakingly long hours of staring at those puzzle pieces was actually worth it all in the end. Big sigh. Big relief.

We humans need to see the end in sight. That's why Jesus was so wonderful to encourage us with verbal pictures of Heaven. If we can endure the pain and trials this world brings, our next one is going to have streets paved with gold! And we humans like gold. And mansions with many rooms. We like mansions. And no more tears. How wonderful will *that* be!

I attended Oral Roberts University in the mid 1980's. I loved my classes, but there was one thing I dreaded. Ask any ORU student from that era. I don't think anyone enjoyed the three mile *mandatory* field test. Every single student had to pass this running test with a good time. And as I believe I told you before, I'm not a great runner. If I could have biked the field test, no problem! But running? And a *timed* race? Ugh.

Every semester the field test took place in a different location. Sometimes on the inside gym track (13 miles around the track equaled only one mile). Sometimes on the outside track, and sometimes they partitioned off a whole road for all the students.

The only saving grace was when I saw the end in sight. At that point I knew I could make it. Again, if it were *un*-timed, I think I would have been fine. But the pressure that if you didn't pass the field test with a good time—you couldn't graduate, was horrid to say the least. Graduating college and the ending point gave me the endurance I needed.

Now I feel wimpy writing all that. What's three miles? Nothing. But when you're in the middle of senior year finals, and all you want to do is get on with your life, it's everything. Seeing goals coming to completion is important. If not, we're just running and running and running. We need to see that finish line. It propels us forward.

Paul talked about the goal of running the race of life so well in Philippians, "I'm not saying that I have this all together, that I have it made. But I am well on my way, reaching out for Christ, who has so wondrously reached out for me. Friends, don't get me wrong: By no means do I count myself an expert in all of this, but I've got my eye on the goal, where God is beckoning us onward—to Jesus. I'm off and running, and I'm not turning back."

Personally, I wouldn't have minded if Paul wrote, "I'm off riding my bicycle to the finish line", but he used the metaphor of running. I think Paul would have liked bicycles. Much more fun. Too bad he lived before they were invented. But I'm sure you get the point of what he was trying to express.

I agree with Paul. I, myself, certainly don't have it all together by any means. That's why I write books that deal with issues I am going through myself. It's my weird form of self-therapy, if you will. I have to study and look up all these topics. And in doing so, I greatly learn, too. But Paul speaks of the deep urge to finish the race.

Why do people even buy puzzles? For the thrill of completing a difficult task? Do we humans enjoy a challenge? I think so. Just not a challenge completely out of our capabilities. If a puzzle *can't* be completed, it's no fun. We ultimately know that all of our time and effort will have been wasted. But if we translate all of our puzzle talk into our everyday lives, we have way more than jigsaw cut pieces to work with.

As Christians, we do have a glimpse of the completed picture. It's to be in Heaven with Jesus for the rest of our soul's existence. We are told that it will have no end. But once we are in Heaven, we don't need to have earthly goals. We'll be residing past the finish line. New rules. New goals. New way of life. Beyond what we can imagine right now.

We lived in Colorado for five years. Five wonderful years of raising our boys in that gloriously beautiful state. Driving east away from the mountains is always a tad sad. You keep peeking in the rear view mirror until you can't see those purple mountain majesty peaks anymore. Then you're stuck with rolling plains for *hours*. But driving west into Colorado is a different story. Especially if you have endured the ridiculously long drive through Kansas beforehand.

There is this anticipation in the car. And a contest. Who will be the first to spot the tips of the mountains? Anyone else play this game? All four of us peering through the front window in hopes to visually spot the Rocky Mountains. It never got old. Always exciting.

We have two other places in America where we do the same sort of thing. The first to spot the Arch when driving through St. Louis, and the first one to see the Epcot 'ball' (Spaceship Earth) when flying into Orlando. It's a Hart family *thing*. The first one to yell, "I see it!" wins. And we all like to win. Even if it's just spotting the St. Louis Arch.

What is the goal that you see? Is it attainable? What are you striving to see come to fruition in your life? Picture your greatest dream. Can you visualize the possibility of it coming true?

I was never a pageant girl. I competed in the Little Miss New Jersey pageant once, because my parents entered me. They're really not my thing. For my talent, I sang Snoopy's 'Suppertime' song from the musical You're A Good Man Charlie Brown. My parents picked it out. I was not well-schooled in the pageant world, obviously.

PUZZLE PIECE LIVING

What I mostly remember about the Little Miss New Jersey pageant was that the girls were so mean. So mean to each other, but especially mean to their mothers. It was not a fit for me. But yet, for years, I enjoyed watching the Miss America pageant. Until they moved it away from Atlantic City. Which I believe was a huge mistake.

People always joke about certain Miss America contestants (in their interview questions) telling the judges and audience that their goal is to have 'world peace'. It sounds so nice. But highly impractical, don't you think? *Can* the world we live in *really* be at 100% peace? Hopefully the goal that you visualize and see is more realistic, and something that can actually take place in your life.

I joke that I want the title Prophetess Kirsten. I have been involved with ministries where the males have the title Prophet, and the women, Prophetess. I'm not totally sure how one attains the status of that title. Are there so many prophecies you have to give that turn out right before that title is officially given to you?

The prophets of the Old Testament were given the gift of seeing into the future. Most prophecies were warnings. Not many prophecies were the pageant answer of 'world peace', much to the contrary. Some of those claiming to be prophets in this day and age are simply wanting to give a sort of fortune telling session to someone. These prophecies consist of more encouraging words, rather than warnings. But I don't want to overstep my boundaries and lack of knowledge with those that claim this spiritual gift from God.

My point in bringing up the prophetic? Wouldn't it be wonderful for someone to give us the full picture of what lies ahead in our futures? So that we could verbally hear the plans God specifically has for us? Wouldn't it make our day to day circumstances so much easier to bear? To have a word from the Lord, giving us our full picture? Telling us what our completed puzzle will look like?

Can you see it? Is it within reach yet? Is the whole picture coming together? Are your corners in place? The main picture clearly visible? Only a few pieces yet to place? Good. Keep on. Completion is near.

Chapter Thoughts

--List three of your greatest life accomplishments. Why are these significant to you?

_____

_____

_____

_____

_____

_____

_____

--Paul mentioned in Philippians that 'I'm not saying I have this all together', referencing his life. What *do* you have 'all together' in your life? What areas of your life need improvement?

_____

_____

_____

_____

_____

_____

_____

--What's the greatest challenge you're currently facing in your life? Why is this a challenge?

_____

_____

_____
_____
_____
_____
_____

--If a true prophet of God told you that he could predict the exact details of your future, would you want that information? Do you think you would live your life differently?

_____
_____
_____
_____
_____
_____
_____

--If you could perfectly plan and predict your own future, what would it look like? Where would you be and what would you be doing in twenty years?

_____
_____
_____
_____
_____
_____
_____

--Are your goals realistic? What elements keep them realistic? What elements are

seemingly far reaching, and not practical?
How can you modify your goals so that
they are attainable? Would you want to
modify, or keep your goals supposedly
ginormous?

_____

_____

_____

_____

_____

_____

_____

Prayer:

God,

Thank you for giving us a true hope and future. We daily place our lives in your hands. Every obstacle that comes our way, and every difficulty we give to you. Make something beautiful out of our lives. We want to give you the glory in every single situation we face. We acknowledge that you are the author of our future. Thank you for keeping us in your hands. We love you.

Amen

Completed

'It ain't over till the fat lady sings.' I've heard that phrase for years, but never really knew what it meant until recently. The musical connection is with the operatic role of Brunnhilde in Richard Wagner's Götterdämmerung (I know. I can't pronounce it either, but it's kind of fun to try to say). Apparently it's an extremely long opera at fourteen *hours* in length! Brunnhilde is usually depicted as a 'well-upholstered' lady who appears for a ten minute solo to finish the opera. When is the opera over? When Brunnhilde (a fat lady) literally sings.

All of that to tell you, your life *ain't over till it's over.* If you're not ready to have your life done, don't let a Brunnhilde come out to sing!

When your puzzle is complete, and every tiny piece has found its appropriate place, then sit back and enjoy what the Lord has for you in your next chapter.

I love telling people "If you woke up this morning, that means the Lord still has purpose for your life". And I believe it. But someday every plan that God has for us while on earth will be completed. I, personally, don't want to go before 100. If I have some mental capacity, and can still function, I'd love to live one hundred years. Just think what I can accomplish in my upcoming years! What adventures the Lord still could have planned for my journey.

I've told a few of my favorite 'saints' before they passed on that I requested they meet me when it's my time to go past the curtain of this world to the next. How 'fun' (I can say fun, right?) to instantly pass from this existence into a new and glorious future. I desire to fulfill my purpose here first, but 'what a day that will be'.

I'm sure you can share the sentiment that I want to be 'used up'. I desire that God 'squeezes' every single ounce of purpose out of me. Our whole lives we are searching for that *exact thing* we were placed on earth to do and be. Most of us spend our whole lives searching for our 'place in this world'. Perhaps our place isn't in *this* world. Just perhaps every single thing we learn here--our wisdom, our training, knowledge, trades, etc. is just preparation for our roles and ultimate calling in Heaven. What if our days here are preparing us for what we will be doing for eternity in Heaven and the new Earth? Isn't that a cool thought?

What if God planted an idea or dream inside of you, because he already had plans for your Heavenly role? He placed a desire inside you to learn what you ultimately will be doing for eternity? If the souls we have here are the same souls we have in Heaven, then we have the capability to take all of our knowledge to Heaven with us, too. I know I'm just speculating here, but *what if?* This is why it's so important that we never give up on the puzzle. It all fits together. There is purpose. There is meaning.

We have such a fascination with what happens to us after we die. Myself included. Because people are dying every single second of every minute. All those people instantly knowing what life after death is like. Instantly. All their questions answered.

I have read most of the books by those who have died and come back to life. They're so fascinating. And I'm intrigued. Even to catch a tiny glimpse 'first hand' by an author that experienced the beyond, is invaluable knowledge. Wouldn't you love to just be able to go to Heaven long enough to come back and tell everyone exact details?

The one book of the Bible that was never included is one that contains all of the stories from the people that were raised from the dead. I would *love* to know what Lazarus experienced for the three days he was dead and gone. It was prior to the resurrection of Jesus, so did he just 'sleep'? Did he experience a sort of purgatory? In Daniel 12:2 the dead are described as those who "sleep in the dust." I think that's a very interesting description. Not very 'gold paved roads and mansions'.

In the Old Testament, we are told that the souls of the departed went to Sheol or Hades, which is not specifically the Hell we are taught about. Sheol and Hades were a places that souls wandered. Not a place of punishment.

I'm not a Heaven/Hell scholar by any means. That's probably obvious. And although I would *love* to know what happened with Lazarus, and all the other dead-to-lifers in the Bible, it simply isn't written. We can only speculate.

Jesus said to the thief on the cross, "Today you will be with me in Paradise". Paradise is an ancient Persian word that means garden. A lovely beautiful garden. And it's a word that was in common use at the time to mean a place of rest and refreshment and delight. But it wasn't the ultimate destination. Because when Jesus tells the thief that 'today' you will be with me, the 'today' was Good Friday. So it would seem that there *was* a place prior to Heaven itself.

Why all this talk about Heaven? Because that is the destination of our reward. When our puzzle of life is completed, we will be finished with our earthly journey, and on to eternity. Why not learn all we can about the place we will be forever? It completely fascinates me. Yet all of us reading this book are still on our earthly path.

It is interesting that Jesus talks a lot about the Kingdom of God, but not necessarily tons of details about Heaven itself. But do some searching on your own if you want. Dig into your Bible to find out more about the reward you have in Heaven. Read the prophets from the Old Testament and the book of Revelation for some more intricate details. It's more than just fascinating. It's your destination.

I recently read that while Steve Jobs (co-founder and CEO of Apple) was dying, his actual final words were, "Wow, wow, wow!" Wouldn't you love to know what he was seeing!

I also read a book written by a hospice nurse, who tells of different stories of people dying. Many times, people that were talking as they were dying have mentioned seeing past loved ones sitting there in their rooms, ready to take them to Heaven. That just makes me smile. We honestly have no idea what lies in our future. Only that it's going to be amazing.

So where are you in your puzzle building? Are you just dumping the pieces out and getting situated? Are you getting your foundational corners set? Are you still searching for those missing pieces?

Keep looking at the box top! Keep the big picture in sight. Don't lose hope and give up. It'll all be worth it in the end!

This is the end of my book, but it's just the beginning of more journeys for you. Perhaps you're just a puzzle beginner. Maybe you've solved more than you care to mention. It's a beautiful expedition, is it not? This life we are privileged to live? Don't take it for granted.

Cling to the hope that God will use every single life experience for good. That's how we make it day to day! Every crazy, beautiful, frustrating, amazing, funny, confusing season in your life will all fit together. [SOMEHOW!]

Enjoy the journey!
Kirsten

Chapter Thoughts

--If you could plan your death, how old would you be, and how would you die?

_____

_____

_____

_____

_____

_____

_____

--In your mind, what would you want Heaven to honestly be like? Would you prefer a mansion, or are you more of a lake cabin person? Would you want to live with *all* of your family members, or just certain ones?

_____

_____

_____

_____

_____

_____

_____

--Have you ever lived through a near-death experience (NDE)? Do you anyone that personally has? What was their story?

_____

_____

_____
_____
_____
_____
_____

--If your current vocation/job was to be your vocation/job for all of eternity in Heaven and the new Earth, would you be happy and fulfilled? If you could choose a vocation to have in Heaven, what would it be?

_____
_____
_____
_____
_____
_____
_____

--Do you believe we instantly go to Heaven when we die? Do our bodies and souls stay in the ground until the Second Coming? What Bible verses prove what you believe?

_____
_____
_____
_____
_____
_____
_____

--From reading the Bible, what do we know for sure about Heaven? What will it look like? What will eternity be like?

_____

_____

_____

_____

_____

_____

_____

--Where are you on your puzzle building journey? Do you feel like most of your pieces are in place? What is still missing in your life? What will it take for your puzzle to be complete?

_____

_____

_____

_____

_____

_____

_____

Prayer:

Jesus,
Thank you so much for these lives you
have given us to live. We praise you.
We love you. We worship you. You
gave us life, and you desire for these lives
of ours to be abundant. We give you our
present and our futures. Take our lives.
Mold them. Shape us to be who we
were created to be. We run this race,
knowing that you are standing at the finish
line. May we all hear the words,
"Well done, good and faithful servant."
Amen

About The Author

Author, speaker, and singer Kirsten Hart has been able to travel with some of America's premier Christian singing groups, including Re-Creation, Eternity, The Spurrlows, FRIENDS (the back-up group for Grammy Award winner Larnelle Harris), The Richard Roberts TV Singers, as a Praise and Worship Leader for International Crusades, on TBN's This Is Your Day telecast, as well as BET TV's Manasseh Jordan Show. Since moving to Branson, Missouri, she has been a part of DINO Kartsonakis' Christmas Spectacular Show, as well as his Tribute To The Titanic production.

She has had the amazing opportunity to sing on television, in hundreds of churches, and as part of international crusades. She has shared her heart before thousands. She also counts it a privilege to have sung for Focus On The Family and Compassion International events, Camp Meetings, Statewide Conventions, and more.

Kirsten has spoken in churches and for Women's Ministry Events across the country for the past twenty years.

www.KirstenHart.com

ALSO AVAILABLE ON AMAZON.COM

Queen Esther was just an ordinary Hebrew girl that God reinvented into a Queen in order to save His people. King David was reinvented from a shepherd boy to a King. Moses was 80 when he was called to lead the nation of Israel.

What does God have yet in store for your life? Explore the possibilities that God has for you in every changing season of your journey.

Newlywed to young mom to empty nester to retirement age--God can transform your life at every stage to use your gifts in ways greater than you could ever imagine. There are no limits to how God can reinvent your life to maximize all of your potential.

Group Study questions for every chapter!

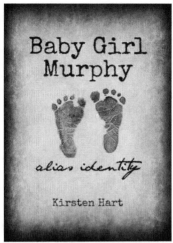

Baby Girl
Murphy

alias identity

Kirsten Hart

"I'm sorry, Mrs. Hart, we don't have any birth records for you." These were the words I heard over the phone when I was trying to locate a copy of my birth certificate for a new passport. "Have you checked with the Adoption Registry Office?" was the following question. Adoption? I was forty-one years old. I knew who my parents were. Why would someone suggest that I talk with an Adoption Registry Office? I just simply needed a copy of my birth certificate. That phone call led me on a new journey of discovery and secrets.

Who was I? Who was my birth mother? Did I have other siblings? What was my story? Baby Girl Murphy is my personal exploration of discovering my new identity and unveiling a secret that God had kept for 41 years. A secret so dear, yet so mysterious. "...Find out more..." were the words I kept hearing echo through my heart. Indeed I did find out more. More than I ever dreamed imaginable.

CHAT is for every small group that enjoys digging into intriguing Biblical topics. Set aside time to grab some snacks and coffee, and journey into a Bible study that seeks to draw out conversations whether in a living room or neighborhood café.

This is not your average small group study. CHAT contains twelve individual topics that aren't successive, yet can be used on a weekly basis. Pick and choose. Jump around. It's up to you.

Designed for busy people with an appetite for truth, and connection with each other and God.

CHAT is for every teen group that enjoys digging into intriguing Biblical topics. Set aside time to grab some snacks and a cappuccino, and journey into a Bible study that seeks to draw out conversations whether in a living room or neighborhood café.

This is not your average small group study. CHAT contains twelve individual topics that aren't successive, yet can be used on a weekly basis. Pick and choose. Jump around. It's up to you. Designed for busy teens with an appetite for truth, and connection with each other and God.

*CHAT Teens is the teen version of CHAT for adults— (the red cup cover). CHAT Teens contains the same chapter topics as the adult version (except for one chapter) just worded for the teen audience. Teens and their parents can dig in, and discuss the same Bible topics at home!

How can avocados, King Solomon, mascara, cat litter, banana peels, little known verses in Proverbs, H2O, Dead Sea Mud, and vegetables all be related? Why, they're all Beauty Secrets! Sound impossible? Want to know more details? I can't tell you here! They're secrets! But they're all revealed inside this book.

Is this book all about make-up? No way. Is this book all about physical health? Not really. This book is a wonderful combination of all the elements that make a woman beautiful from her heart and health to her style she reveals to the world. Cat litter? How does cat litter fit into a Beauty Book? You'd be surprised! But I can't tell you! It's a SECRET!

CHAT Christmas is a special edition of the CHAT 'A Conversational Bible Study' series. Usually the CHAT books contain twelve separate chapters. This Christmas edition only contains four, and is meant as a special study to fit in-between Thanksgiving and Christmas. Designed to concentrate on this time of celebrating Thanksgiving and the birth of our Lord.

CHAT was designed not to be a right or wrong answer conversational Bible study. No questions to fill in. And if you miss a week, you can't get behind. Every week has a non-chronological different topic of discussion. Grab a cup of coffee, a snack, and dig into challenging topics with your small group.

49327418R00078

Made in the USA
Columbia, SC
20 January 2019